PREPARING FOR PROMOTION AND TENURE REVIEW

PREPARING FOR PROMOTION AND TENURE REVIEW

A Faculty Guide

Robert M. Diamond
Syracuse University

Anker Publishing Company, Inc.
Bolton, MA

PREPARING FOR PROMOTION AND TENURE REVIEW
A Faculty Guide

ISBN 1-882982-07-X

Composition by Deerfoot Studios
Cover design by Deerfoot Studios

Anker Publishing Company, Inc.
176 Ballville Road
P.O. Box 249
Bolton, MA 01740-0249

About the Author

Robert M. Diamond is Assistant Vice Chancellor, Director of the Center for Instructional Development, and Professor of Instructional Design, Development & Evaluation, and Higher Education at Syracuse University, and is Director of the National Project on Institutional Priorities and Faculty Rewards funded by the Lilly Endowment and the Pew Charitable Trusts. Diamond coauthored the 1987 National Study of Teaching Assistants, the 1992 National Study of Research Universities on the Balance Between Research and Undergraduate Teaching, and was responsible for the design and implementation of Syracuse University's award-winning high school/college transition program, Project Advance. He is also codirector of the Syracuse University Focus on Teaching Project. Dr. Diamond is author of *Serving on Promotion and Tenure Committees: A Faculty Guide* (Anker, 1994), has published extensively, and is a consultant to colleges and universities throughout the world.

CONTENTS

About the Author   *v*

Acknowledgments   *ix*

Part I
Process

Introduction   2

1. Planning Ahead   4

    Know the Rules: Procedures and Criteria   4

    Collect Other Useful Information   6

    Develop a Focused Interest or a
        Specific Line of Research   9

    Document Special Assignments   9

    Collect Baseline Data   10

    Recognize the Unusual Challenges You May Face   11

    Recognize the Importance of Interpersonal Relations   12

    Keep Your Vitae Up-to-Date   12

    Get Help   13

2. Documenting Your Work   14

    What Constitutes Faculty Work?   14

    Documenting Teaching Effectiveness   15

    Documenting Advising Effectiveness   20

    Documenting Service Activities   21

    Documenting Scholarly, Professional, and
        Creative Work   21

    The Professional Portfolio   22

    The Faculty Essay   24

    Examples of Documentation   25

3. In Summary   26

    References   27

Part II
Resources

4. The Disciplines Consider Scholarship   30

    The American Historical Association   31

    The American Assembly of Collegiate Schools of
      Business   33

    The Work of the Theater Faculty   35

    The American Chemical Society   37

    The Joint Policy Board for Mathematics   38

    The American Academy of Religion   41

    The Association of American Geographers   46

5. Student Ratings of Faculty: Special Instructional Settings   52

6. Evaluating Teaching: Selected Additional References   54

7. Evaluating an Advisor: ACT Survey of
    Academic Advising   56

8. Documenting and Assessing Work of Faculty   57

    Author Textbook as Introduction to the Discipline   57

    Develop New High School Curriculum   59

    Direct a Play (Student Production)   60

    Design a New Course   61

    Serve on Community Task Force   63

    Assist Regional Museum in Producing an Exhibit   65

    Develop Software to Model Environmental Effects   66

9. Preparing for Promotion and Tenure:
    A Faculty Checklist   67

Acknowledgments

I would like to thank the following colleagues for their excellent feedback and suggestions as this guide was being drafted: Bronwyn Adam, Lou Albert, Bill Bayliss, Paula Brownlee, Ron Cavanagh, Kim Dittus, Sandra Elman, Don Ely, Jim Gardner, Rachael Hendrickson, Sam Hope, Bob Jensen, Bill Laidlaw, Gene Rice, Robert Rubinstein, Rich Sours, Toni Toland, Mark Whitney, and Assate Zerai.

This guide has been developed as part of the Syracuse University National Project on Institutional Priorities and Faculty Rewards funded in part by the Lilly Endowment, Inc., The Pew Charitable Trusts, and the Fund for the Improvement of Postsecondary Education

PART I

PROCESS

INTRODUCTION

One of the most difficult and challenging experiences you will have in your career as a faculty member is the process of preparing for promotion and/or tenure review. While typically your first formal review will be for both tenure and promotion, there are situations in which the review for promotion is independent. This guide has been prepared to assist you in preparing for either. In it we have included materials appropriate for faculty at large universities and small colleges, public and private institutions, and unionized campuses. Settings do indeed vary; however, the questions that need to be considered and the materials you will need to collect are basically the same across contexts. What will vary considerably are the policies and practices for review, the procedures followed, the criteria applied to evaluate your work, the weight given to specific activities, and the extent to which assistance is provided along the way through formal institutional channels or networks.

A number of initiatives are underway on campuses and in national associations to make the promotion and tenure process more fair to candidates and more closely aligned with the priorities of departments and institutions. Guidelines are being clarified, techniques for documenting faculty work are being developed, and, in a growing number of departments, experienced and respected faculty members are being asked to work with new faculty members as mentors. In addition, there is a growing body of literature on the subject of faculty evaluation and assessment.

As a candidate for promotion or tenure, perhaps the most important thing for you to realize is that there are a number of things you can do, almost from the first day of your appointment, to improve your chances of a positive review. The more you know about the process and timeline that will be followed on your campus and in your department, the criteria that will be used, and the ways in which you can document your accomplishments, the greater your chances for success. You have an important role to play in determining the focus of your review and in selecting those materials that will be reviewed by the promotion and/or tenure committee.

This guide has been developed to assist you by enumerating important questions you should ask and the issues you should consider as you approach your review. Included are some suggestions concerning the materials that you will submit for review. You will also find specific examples illustrating how you might document the impact of your professional work as well as a review of the data and support materials you could provide. Keep in mind that there is no single format or best approach. Every promotion and tenure review is bound by its context. Yours will be determined by the guidelines and procedures of your department, school, college or institution, by the campus culture, by the specific assignments you have undertaken, and by your own set of interests and priorities. In this guide the focus is on process—on what you can do to make a better case for why you should be promoted or tenured.

1

PLANNING AHEAD

The more complete the information you have about the promotion and tenure process at your institution, the better. As you read this guide, it is important to keep in mind that criteria and procedures vary from institution to institution, from discipline to discipline, and from department to department. While in a larger institution there may be several committees involved (often at the department, school/college, and institution level), in a smaller institution there is apt to be a single promotion and tenure committee reporting directly to the provost or academic vice-president. Remember also that at some point in the process those reviewing your materials will be from other academic disciplines. This is a key factor that you will have to consider when you prepare your documentation. You will also find a difference in focus between promotion and tenure committees. While promotion committees tend to base their decision on past accomplishments, tenure committees will consider both past performance and your long-term future, i.e., what you can contribute to the unit and to the institution in the years ahead. Start early to prepare for your review. Long before the actual date of your final review, there are a number of steps you can take.

Know the Rules: Procedures and Criteria
What You Should Know
Shortly after your faculty appointment, you should begin to gather information in five general areas.

1. *The review process in your unit*

    - Is there an annual review procedure? Is this a formal or informal review process? What is required?

- Is there a more comprehensive three-year review? How is it similar or different in process and practice from the tenure review?

2. *The type of documentation the committee will expect*

    - What materials does the committee expect you to provide to document your teaching, research or scholarship, and service activities?

    - If a professional or teaching portfolio is expected or encouraged, what should be included, and how should it be organized and presented?

    - Will you be asked to provide copies of publications? Will you be asked to provide published reviews of these publications? Will you be asked to solicit other reviews?

    - Should you provide letters of support and, if so, from whom and how many?

    - Should you provide a list of references, and, if so, when?

    - How much material should be presented and on what timeline?

3. *The specific steps that will be followed by the committee(s)*

    - What steps will the committee follow, and what is the anticipated timeline?

    - Will the committee interview other colleagues?

    - Will documentation or assessment be requested from individuals outside the institution?

    - How will these external reviewers be selected, and what will they be asked to do?

    - Are you expected to provide nominations for outside reviewers? If so, select these individuals with great care, making sure that they hold positions that indicate recognition in their field in addition to disciplinary expertise.

4. *The criteria that will be used to assess the quality of the materials that are provided*

    - Publications, for example, can be reviewed in many ways. Will they simply be counted using some formula for weighting, or will a sample be reviewed against a specific set of standards? How are different publications weighted? Which are the "valued" publications in your discipline and in your department?

- How will the quality of teaching or advising be determined, and how will the quality and significance of other professional activities be measured?

5. *The relative weighting of various activities*

- Is there a set formula for determining the importance of specific functions, or will these be considered on an individual basis according to assignment?

- Is there a particular approach for determining the relative weight of activities? e.g., 40 percent on the quality of teaching, 40 percent research, and 20 percent service.

Information of this nature may be provided to you by your department or program chair or by another designated mentor. At many institutions, the communication of this information is part of a formal three-year review process. If preparatory information is not provided to you, ask for it. Your institution or department may not have addressed some of these questions or issues. If that is the case, it will be up to you to prepare for the committee a file of materials that makes the best case for the quality of your work. Keep in mind that policies or practices at your institution may change. Be sure that you are informed of any modifications in guidelines or procedures if such changes apply to you. It may be that, despite changes, your case will be judged by the policies or criteria that were in place at the time you were hired.

Collect Other Useful Information

There are several formal documents that will prove helpful to you as you begin to describe, define, and document the quality and significance of your work:

- Your institutional mission statement
- Your school/college, or departmental mission or priority statements
- A statement from your discipline describing the work of faculty in your field

- On unionized campuses, the sections of the collective bargaining agreement related to promotion and tenure procedures and criteria
- Regional accreditation standards (these associations and agencies are increasingly including promotion and tenure guidelines in their criteria)

Mission Statements

The more closely your work relates to the stated missions of your institution, school/college, or department, the greater weight is apt to be applied to that work in your review. In recent years a growing number of institutions have clarified their mission statements with schools, colleges, and departments describing their priorities in detail and relating their promotion, tenure, and merit guidelines to these priorities. It will be up to you to relate the materials you present to what the institution says it values, making the case for your work as a manifestation of institutional goals. Since department missions can vary significantly, explication of your practice as it relates to the priorities of your academic unit is important information for the committee to have.

A Statement from Your Discipline

As you prepare your materials, remember that there are major differences among the disciplines, both in terms of faculty practice and methodology and in the language used to describe faculty work. These differences can be problematic when a faculty member comes up for review by colleagues from other disciplines, particularly if the work presented does not take the form of traditional research and publication.

To provide assistance in the assessment of faculty work, a number of disciplinary associations have participated in a project coordinated at Syracuse University (sponsored by the Fund for the Improvement of Postsecondary Education and the Lilly Endowment) to develop comprehensive statements describing the scholarly and professional work in their respective fields. These statements provide valuable insights for those confronting the discipline-specific nature of scholarship. In Chapter 4 you will find brief segments from several statements as well as information about obtaining the full documents.

If you are not aware of such a statement for your discipline, write to the national office of the major scholarly society or accreditation agency for faculty in your field, and ask if such a document exists. Statements from your disciplinary association can prove to be extremely helpful as you document the significance of your scholarly and professional work. The full statements from a number of disciplines including Architecture, Art and Design, Business, Chemistry, Dance, Family and Consumer Studies, Geography, Geology, History, Journalism Landscape Architecture, Mathematics, Music, Religion, Sociology, and Theater have been published in a single volume, *Statements From the Disciplines,* by the American Association for Higher Education, One Dupont Circle, Suite 360, Washington, DC 20036.

Options Available to You

As a faculty member approaching tenure, there may be several options available to you. In an increasing number of institutions, faculty are being given the opportunity to negotiate the weighting that will be applied to their various activities (teaching, research, service, citizenship, or outreach, etc.) prior to review. This practice acknowledges the individual differences of faculty and the need to consider review on a case-by-case basis.

You may have the option of taking a leave of absence or reduced teaching load in order to prepare for your review. In some situations there may be an option of "stopping the tenure clock" so as to give you adequate time to prepare your case. Investigate all these options with your department chair or dean. Taking advantage of additional time to carefully prepare your case can make a significant difference in the outcome.

The Collective Bargaining Agreement

If you work on a unionized campus, a review of the collective bargaining agreement can be helpful. Such contracts typically address evaluation procedures, specific timelines, and the composition of review committees, among other particulars. For a discussion of tenure prepared from the union perspective, see *Entering the Profession: Advice for the Untenured,* published by the National Education Association, 1201 16th Street, NW, Washington, DC 20036.

The Formal Appeal Process

Every institution has a formal appeal process to which faculty can turn for review of a negative decision. This process will usually be described in your faculty handbook or collective bargaining agreement.

Develop a Focused Interest or a Specific Line of Research

Promotion and tenure committees look for evidence of sustained inquiry—of depth and long-term disciplinary commitment that centers and integrates one's professional work. It is important that you develop a specialty or area of expertise that is appropriate for your field and your long term goals and that you can articulate it clearly. As you move ahead, you will need to document the full scope of your activity and the significance of it. Focus on how your work is making a contribution to your field. If articles or research reports are appropriate, aim at having them published in refereed journals. If you are in the creative arts, have your work peer reviewed in exhibitions or by experts in the field. Consider developing presentations in your area of specialization for regional and national meetings. Also find ways of relating your work to your teaching and, if possible, have students join you as you pursue your line of inquiry. Your documentation in this area will provide the basis for the committee's review of the scholarly/professional/creative dimension of your work.

Document Special Assignments

While most institutions try to avoid giving new faculty members assignments that constrain their ability to devote time to the more traditional activities of research and publication, there are exceptions. You may be asked or even required to participate in specific projects, be involved in major course or curriculum design activities, or assume a number of administrative responsibilities. These can affect your promotion and tenure in three ways. First, such responsibilities can impinge on the range of activities that you can realistically perform. Second, such work can impact on the time you have available to conduct research, prepare publications, attempt innovations in your teaching, or perform service in your institution or community. Third, these activities can be recognized as "scholarly and professional" work by your department. If a special assignment will not be recognized in your review and will impinge on your time to a significant degree, you should discuss with your department chair possibilities for adjusting your tenure clock (i.e., how many years you have before a formal review is required.) Request that the assignment and related expectations and activities be put in writing and filed in your personnel folder. If such assignments and conditions are included in your appointment letter, make sure that this document is also in your file. You may want to refer to them later as you describe the focus of your work and the constraints under which you were working.

Collect Baseline Data

In the years prior to your review for promotion or tenure, many events and experiences will provide opportunities for personal growth and professional development. Documenting those activities may prove to be invaluable as you approach tenure or promotion review. You may be asked to address a problem identified in your work, perhaps at the time of an earlier review. (Many institutions are now implementing a required in-depth review of all faculty during their third year of appointment for the specific reason of helping them prepare for their tenure review.) You may want to experiment with some innovative instructional strategy in a class to address concerns you have, or you may make major changes in the content of a course for instructional improvement. In such instances, you will want to collect data on the problem before you do anything. Such baseline data might consist of student responses to the current curriculum, comments from alumni or employers, student grades over time, attrition data, or any information that helps identify the problem you perceive.

If you are active in community-related projects, look for reports or surveys that articulate the problem you plan to address. There may be articles in professional journals that provide a strong rationale for the work you want to pursue. All of these sources can be incorporated as documentation when you present your case. Look for data that can be useful as you attempt to show the positive impact your work has had. As you plan changes in your work with students or in your scholarship, you need to consider potential outcomes. You may want to ask yourself the question, "If I am successful, what will change, how will it change, and how can I document this change?"

Recognize the Unusual Challenges that You May Face

Most faculty serving on promotion and tenure committees will be comfortable with the documentation associated with research and scholarly publication. A growing number will also be familiar with the various means of assessing and documenting good teaching. There are, however, several areas where problems of multiple interpretations and values typically arise.

The definition of what is scholarly and professional work

There is no single, agreed upon definition of what is meant by the term "scholarship." Some disciplines avoid the word altogether, preferring instead "professional work" or "intellectual contribution." Each discipline has its own definition, and it may not be articulated in a formal document. In order to help your reviewers to understand the quality of your work, you may need to provide the committee with the definition of scholarship or professional work you follow. Disciplinary statements can support your rationale for the scholarly and professional nature of your work.

New and developing disciplines

If you are in one of the newer academic areas such as Women's Studies or African-American Studies, you face a unique challenge. In new disciplines, a research history or tradition may not exist and publication outlets may be limited. In addition, much of the documentation that does exist may appear in non-traditional forms such as video, audio histories, or in publications that do not have clearly established traditions. Some committee members may be unfamiliar with your field. It will be up to you to provide them with a rationale and documentation that they can understand, appreciate, and assess. Find out how leading educators in your field on other campuses have addressed these issues and learn from them.

Interdisciplinary or collaborative work

Just as faculty in newer disciplines face challenges, so do faculty involved in interdisciplinary or collaborative work. Increasing thought is being given to the assessment of work produced by coauthors, or investigators—teams that may consist of faculty from more than one discipline or experts from the community. While the overall success of your work will have to be documented, it will be your responsibility to describe and assess your role within the group and the impact that you had on the outcome of the collaboration. If you are working in an interdisciplinary context, take particular care to relate your work to your own discipline and to the priorities of your department and institution.

Changes in leadership

Appointment of a new department chair, dean, or administrator can precipitate a radical change in promotion and tenure policies or practices. Such changes can evolve over time or be quite sudden. Whenever significant change occurs, you need to pay particular attention to any statements regarding promotion and tenure review. If new policies seem quite different from written statements in effect previously or from particular agreements you negotiated, address this difference with your department chair or unit head immediately.

Recognize the Importance of Interpersonal Relations

Remember that promotion and tenure is a political process involving the attitudes and perceptions of committee members, argument and deliberation components, and formal and informal voting. Citizenship is becoming increasingly important as a criterion for tenure. Even with strong credentials, you may be refused tenure if you are perceived as being uncooperative or uninterested in working with colleagues in your department. For a discussion of the political nature of the faculty review process, see *Getting Tenure* by Whicker, Kronenfeld, and Strickland.

Keep Your Vitae Up-to-Date

Begin collecting materials for your dossier early, and update your vitae on a regular basis. From the day of your appointment, begin filing important documents that could prove useful later on. As your file expands, you can begin organizing your materials in any number of ways. The materials you submit to the review committee will not include all of the documents and materials you collect; however, you can't decide which materials to present until much later. Keep everything! This strategy provides you with a wide array of materials to select from later. A computer makes keeping your vitae up-to-date relatively simple.

Noting on an annual or semi-annual basis the titles and dates for courses taught, special assignments, papers, presentations, and awards will keep your records complete and current. Deleting items later on is much easier than trying to recall particulars four years down the road.

Get Help

As you start preparing your materials, ask a colleague to review them for you, attending to both clarity and completeness. This person may be your mentor or another faculty member whose judgment you trust. It is particularly helpful to find a person who has served on a promotion and tenure committee at your institution. If you are on a campus where the initial committee is cross-disciplinary, having someone from another department who is not familiar with your field might be helpful. The individual can also help by identifying areas in which official policy and actual practice have diverged in recent history. Does institutional rhetoric reflect reality? Getting this anecdotal information is crucial to understanding the culture of your institution and how it affects promotion and tenure review.

In this section we have discussed some of the things you can do from the day of your appointment to help prepare for your promotion or tenure review. In Part II, we will focus on the materials you can present for review.

2

DOCUMENTING YOUR WORK

The promotion and tenure review has basically three components: the documentation that the candidate provides, the material that the committee collects, and the process by which the committee reviews these materials and conducts its deliberations. A well-prepared faculty member can go a long way in making his or her "case" by providing a strong context and solid documentation for the committee to consider.

What Constitutes Faculty Work?

Many descriptions of the work of faculty have been suggested as alternatives to the traditional three-part model of teaching, research, and service. One such expanded taxonomy identifies the following as common discipline-based faculty activities (Gray, et al 1994).

Scholarly activity involving:

- Research that leads to the production of intellectual and/or creative works
- Writing for publication, presentation, or performance

Working with students in many different settings and using many different methods for:

- Teaching undergraduates and graduates
- Advising pre-freshmen to post-doctoral fellows

Citizenship (non-disciplinary):

- Serving on departmental, school, or institutional committees
- Assuming leadership roles within the institution and in professional organizations

- Representing the institution on external committees, task forces, commissions, etc.

Professional service through the application of:

- Disciplinary expertise to assist the institution, citizen groups, government agencies, business, industry

As the candidate, it is your responsibility to describe the range of activities in which you have been engaged and to provide the committee with supportive materials that will help them judge *both* the quality and significance of your work. While the documentation of research and publication has become fairly standardized, demonstration of quality work in other domains is just beginning to receive attention. While some data will be collected by the committee, there is a wide range of information that you should collect and include in the materials that you forward for review.

Documenting Teaching Effectiveness

In the evaluation of teaching, three basic questions must be addressed:

1. Which characteristics will be evaluated?
2. How will data be collected?
3. Who will do the evaluation?

Under each question, a number of options exist (see Table 1).

Student Ratings

Although more comprehensive assessment strategies are now emerging, evaluation of teaching has depended heavily on student ratings. Such measures, while useful, provide only one vision of teacher effectiveness. You should keep in mind that student evaluations are usually collected near the end of the term when many of the failing or unhappy students are no longer in attendance or when those who have remained in class are anxious about final grades. Rather than depending solely on student evaluations to demonstrate your effectiveness in the classroom, think about materials you can collect over time that will demonstrate your growth as a teacher and will display the dynamic nature of the learning enterprise. Course syllabi, assignments and other handouts, student papers, and external

TABLE 1
Planning for Evaluating Teaching

Which characteristics will be evaluated?

- Good organization of subject matter and course
- Effective communication
- Knowledge of and enthusiasm for the subject matter and teaching
- Positive attitudes toward students
- Fairness in assessment and grading
- Flexibility in approaches to teaching
- Appropriate student learning outcomes

↓

How will data be collected?

- Self-assessment/report
- Classroom observation
- Structured interview
- Instructional rating survey
- Test or appraisal of student achievement
- Content analysis of instructional materials
- Review of classroom records

↓

Who will do the evaluating?

- Self
- Students
- Faculty
- Dean or department chair
- Alumni
- Other appropriate administrators

from: John, R.C., Froh, R.C., Gray, P.J., Lambert. L.M. In R. M. Diamond (Ed.). (1987). *A guide to evaluating teaching for promotion and tenure.* Acton, MA: Copley Publishing.

review of student performance or progress can all be used to demonstrate facets of your teaching.

As you collect information about your teaching, remember that student ratings of your teaching can be used to help you improve your effectiveness while at the same time showing that (a) you have worked to become a better teacher and (b) you have collected evidence to show improvement. For example, administering an evaluation instrument mid-semester can provide you with useful information that also shows your students that you care about their progress. This practice offers you the opportunity to make immediate changes in your teaching. Using the same instrument at the end of the semester, or at the same time the following year, can provide evidence of improvement.

Most student rating scales are focused on the lecture as an instructional model. If you are teaching seminar, studio, laboratory, or independent study courses, make sure that inappropriate questions are dropped from student evaluation instruments and replaced with items that address the type of teaching you do. In Chapter 5, you will find examples of questions that might be added for different instructional settings.

The role of teacher as lecturer and "deliverer of knowledge" is an anachronism in many institutions or contexts. As the nature of teaching shifts, the data that will substantiate or document your teaching must shift as well. References focused on evaluating teaching and the use of the teaching portfolio will be found in Chapter 6.

Comparative Ratings

If you are going to use student ratings to help show the quality of your teaching, it is very important that you compare your data on an item by item basis with the averages for other faculty in your department, school/college, or institution. Since most faculty score "above average" responses, providing these data without comparative information is not particularly meaningful. You should be able to get your department, school/college, or institution means from your chair, dean, or the office that does the processing. A simple graphic can effectively be used to present this information.

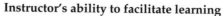

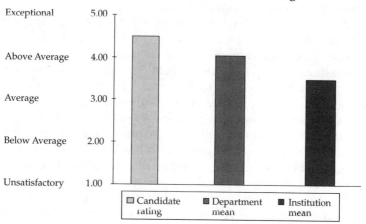

Teacher-Constructed Materials

If you are experimenting with a new instructional approach or have developed new materials for use in your course, another type of instrument can provide you (and later the review committee) with useful information. This instrument, the "mini-quest," (see next page) is given to students immediately after an assignment. The items can be adjusted to meet the needs of the specific materials you are evaluating. Repeated use of this instrument provides feedback on the quality of the instructional materials and helps to document change over time as you revise the approach or materials.

MINI-QUEST
Questionnaire for Evaluation of Materials

Student Evaluation of Materials

Date _____   Material Title _____

Course Title _____   Instructor_____

Please circle the most appropriate alternative.

1. INTEREST
   These materials were:
   (1) very uninteresting
   (2) uninteresting
   (3) interesting
   (4) very interesting

2. PACE
   These materials were:
   (1) much too fast
   (2) a little too fast
   (3) just right
   (4) a little too slow
   (5) much too slow

3. LEARNED
   I learned:
   (1) nothing
   (2) very little
   (3) a fair amount
   (4) a great deal

4. CLARITY
   These materials were:
   (1) very unclear
   (2) unclear
   (3) clear
   (4) very clear

5. IMPORTANCE
   What I learned was:
   (1) very unimportant
   (2) unimportant
   (3) important
   (4) very important

6. GENERAL
   Generally, these materials were:
   (1) poor
   (2) fair
   (3) good
   (4) excellent

7. Please indicate any questions raised by these materials.

8. Please write at least one specific comment here about the materials. (Use the back if necessary.)

Thank you!

from:Diamond, R.M. (1989). *Designing and improving courses and curricula in higher education*. San Francisco, CA: Jossey-Bass.

Documenting Student Learning

It is interesting to note that few faculty include in their documentation evidence of student learning—what Peter Seldin calls the "products of good teaching." Such evidence can be some of the most powerful information you can provide. While the dynamic nature of learning makes documentation complicated, it can be done. You should make every attempt to document the learning that has taken place in your classroom. There are a number of things you can do in this area. If, for example, you have included statements of learning outcomes in your syllabus or course materials, how successful are your students in reaching these objectives? What changes have occurred over time? How has student performance improved? The key question to ask yourself is, "If I am successful as a teacher, what impact will it have on my students and what evidence can I present to demonstrate this impact?"

Documenting Other Impact on Students

As a faculty member, your teaching can have an impact on students in a variety of domains that can also be documented. For example, has there been an increase in your course enrollment? Has attrition decreased? Have attitudes changed? If you have been involved in a major curriculum revision, has there been an impact on job placement or certification performance or in student placement in graduate schools? If you teach an introductory course, have there been changes in students' success in subsequent courses in your discipline? Has enrollment in these courses increased? Has the number of majors increased? What do other faculty say? The answer to each of these question can be included in the data you provide the committee.

Documenting Advising Effectiveness

While the weight given to advising effectiveness may vary considerably from case to case, it is a common category of faculty work and one for which methods of determining success have been developed. One segment of a student survey on academic advising, available through the ACT, is found in Part II-4. As with any survey instrument of this type, it is advisable that it be used over time so that you can benefit from the information as part of formative evaluation. For summative purposes, this information can provide documentation of development in particular areas such as student perceptions as to the quality of the advising they received, your availability, and your concern for their education.

Documenting Service Activities

While many faculty activities fall under the category of "citizenship," the focus of the documentation must be on the importance of the activities and the quality of the work being performed. The weight given to these activities may vary considerably based on your assignment, the significance of the activity, and the relative weight customarily given to this type of work in promotion and tenure cases on your campus.

Depending upon disciplinary practice and institutional and unit missions, "outreach" may be assessed as part of the service or scholarly domains of your work. As the following section suggests, the scholarly aspects of such work should not be overlooked.

Documenting Scholarly, Professional, and Creative Work

Whether it be conducting research, developing a new course, writing a text, implementing an outreach program in the community, directing a play, or assisting in the public schools to improve an academic program, there are many activities that faculty perform that meet the scholarly/professional/creative dimensions required for promotion and tenure. The importance placed on a specific activity will vary from case to case; however, six specific conditions seem to typify most "scholarly" or "professional" activities.

The Basic Features of Scholarly and Professional Work

1. The activity requires a high level of discipline-related expertise.

2. The activity breaks new ground, is innovative.

3. The activity can be replicated or elaborated.

4. The work and its results can be documented.

5. The work and its results can be peer-reviewed.

6. The activity has significance or impact.

---

from Diamond, R., & Adam, B. (1993). *Recognizing faculty work: Reward systems for the year 2000.* San Francisco, CA: Jossey-Bass.

As the candidate, it is your responsibility to provide to the committee materials that substantiate the significance and the quality of your work. It is a mistake to expect the committee to do this for you or to assume that the quality or importance of your work is self-evident.

Some institutions have published statements or guides that facilitate the representation of activities that are of particular importance in light of institutional missions. For example, the Office of Continuing Education and Public Service at the University of Illinois at Urbana-Champaign has published *A Faculty Guide for Relating Public Service to the Promotion and Tenure Review Process.*[1] Materials of this type that discuss criteria, documentation, and evaluation in the context of the specific values of the institution can be extremely helpful to faculty members preparing for review and to the members of review committees.

The Professional Portfolio

Unlike a teaching portfolio, the "professional portfolio" draws together the work a faculty member has done in various domains and presents an overview of a teacher/scholar's best practice. The professional portfolio is a carefully constructed and organized set of materials that represents the full range of faculty work. It begins with a reflective essay (described in the following section) and is structured in such a way to assist the committee in understanding your accomplishments and their significance. Documentation of your work in any portfolio should stress two dimensions: (1) the quality of the work and (2) the significance of the work. Faculty may provide promotion and tenure committees with detailed information as to the quality of their effort but neglect to present a case for the value of their work, describing its impact or explaining in what ways and for whom this work has significance. There is a growing inclination on the part of committees to focus on why the activity was undertaken in the first place and why it is important.

---

[1] Single copies are available at no charge by writing to the Office of Continuing Education and Public Service, the University of Illinois, 302 E. John Street, Suite 202, Champaign, IL 61820

Portfolio documents can be collected from a number of sources. What is important is that the material be focused and manageable. A "selected" professional portfolio provides a selection of materials that can be reviewed in-depth. However, before you take this tack make sure it will meet the expectations of your committee.

A list of potential sources of documentation will be found in Table 2. Notice that while the committee may request additional information in certain categories, you can provide documentation in every one.

TABLE 2
Sources of Documentation (Some Examples)

Establishing Quality
- Expert testimony (formal reviews, juries, and solicited testimony)
- Faculty essay (describing the process that was followed, the rationale behind the decisions that were made, and the quality of the products)
- Formal reports and studies
- Publication, display, or presentation (video based)

Establishing Significance
- Faculty essay (explaining why the work is important, to whom, and for what purposes)
- External reviews focusing on the significance and usefulness of the activity or product
- Impact on the intended audience
    — size and scope
    — documentation (changes in learning, attitudes, performance)
- Relation to the mission statement of the institution/department
- Documentation of individual assignment (what is the department requiring of the faculty member?)
- Disciplinary statement reinforcing type of work involved

The Faculty Essay

One excellent source of information for the review committee is a reflective statement that you prepare as the initial document in your materials. While this descriptive essay may have a number of functions, its primary purpose is to provide a frame of reference or context for the items submitted to the committee. It describes what you see as your priorities and strengths. It states your case. Most importantly, the descriptive essay provides important information to the committee that would not otherwise be available, such as:

- A description of issues from your perspective
- A rationale for choices that you made
- The extent to which your expectations were met
- Circumstances that promoted or inhibited success
- The significance of this work as an intellectual contribution, from your perspective
- An organizational framework for the materials you are submitting

For example, if you have written a textbook, how is it different from other textbooks on the market and why is this an important distinction? If you have directed a play, what specific issues were you addressing, and how is your solution different; why is this important? If you were trying something new, why was this effort important, and if it was not completely successful, what did you learn and how would you modify what you did? Keep in mind that you are the *only* source for this information.

The faculty essay can also serve as the basis for the specific questions that the committee will ask of external reviewers, thus focusing their attention on the issues you and the committee feel are most important. The essay can be used as a descriptive document that provides a rationale for the materials that you have forwarded to the committee and is one way for you to demonstrate a capacity to be reflective and self-critical; hence capable of continued growth and change.

The faculty essay also provides a vehicle for discussion of special circumstances that have affected your work to-date or its review. If, for example, you have been caught in a political struggle within your department and you believe this dispute led to mixed reviews of your work by your colleagues, you may want to address this situation in your essay. Since such disclosures have associated risks, think your decision through carefully. In certain situations, such discussions can advance your case by providing insight your reviewers would not otherwise glean.

It is important, however, to remember the distinction between the descriptive essay and the work itself. You will be judged on the quality of your work. The descriptive essay enhances reviewers' understanding of the work, but does not replace it or its documentation. It may also prove helpful to ask a colleague to review and edit your essay as well as any other documents you have written. Often a fresh pair of eyes can pick up obvious but overlooked errors.

Examples of Documentation

As part of a national project, Institutional Priorities and Faculty Rewards, coordinated at Syracuse University, faculty teams from several campuses and a range of disciplines considered a number of cases and suggested ways in which specific activities might be documented for promotion and tenure review. Several such examples will be found in Chapter 8. As you review these examples, please keep in mind that they are illustrative and not intended to be prescriptive in their detail. You may want to ask your department head or union representative if any examples of successful documentation forms or strategies are available for you to consult. Some departments are collecting review materials to share with faculty as part of a mentoring plan.

3

IN SUMMARY

Preparing for promotion and tenure review is not an easy task. It takes time, planning, and a great deal of hard work. You can be sure that your colleagues on the committee will try to be as fair and supportive as possible. As the candidate, you have the opportunity to help them in their role by providing them with a carefully constructed collection of materials on which to base their decision.

If your campus has a three-year review, use it as a base for the full review that will take place several years later. The comments and advice you receive can prove to be extremely helpful as you move ahead. As hard as some comments may be to take, remember that the purpose of the review is to guide you. For example, a teaching practice that did not work at first can be a valuable asset if you show that you identified a problem or issue, dealt with it, and succeeded in learning from it. If you are fortunate enough to have a senior faculty member serving as your mentor, ask questions, get reactions, and make maximum use of this most valuable resource. Don't lose sight of the fact that the success of your review is, for the most part, in your hands. Be proactive, start collecting your data early, identify the questions you might be asked, and begin to build your case early. Preparing for review is an ongoing process. Remember your audience. Prepare your materials so that they can be understood and appreciated by anyone who is asked to review them.

While preparing for personnel reviews is never an easy task, you can make the process less stressful and more productive by being prepared. Your future in higher education is in your hands. I wish you well.

References

A faculty guide for relating public service to the promotion and tenure review process. (1993). Urbana, IL:University of Illinois at Urbana-Champaign, Office of Continuing Education and Public Service.

American Historical Association Ad hoc Committee on Redefining Scholarly Work. (1994). *Redefining historical scholarship.* Washington, DC: American Historical Association.

Centra, J., Froh, R. C., Gray, P.J., & Lambert, L.M. (1987) In R. M. Diamond, (Ed.). *A guide to evaluating teaching for promotion and tenure.* Acton, MA: Copley. (Available from the Center for Instructional Development, Syracuse University, Syracuse, NY 13244)

Diamond, R.M., & Adam, B.E. (1993). *New Directions in Higher Education. No. 81. Recognizing faculty work: Reward systems for the year 2000.* San Francisco, CA: Jossey-Bass.

Entering the profession: Advice for the untenured. (1994). Washington, DC: National Education Association.

Gray, P., Adam, B., Diamond, R., Froh, R., & Yonai, B. In M. Kinnick (Ed.). (Monograph manuscript in progress). Defining, assigning, and assessing faculty work. *New Directions in Institutional Research. Providing useful information for deans and department chairs.* San Francisco, CA: Jossey-Bass.

Seldin, P. *Successful use of teaching portfolios.* (1993). Bolton, MA: Anker.

Whicker, M. L., Kronenfeld, J.J., & Strickland, R.A. (1993). *Getting tenure.* Newbury Park, CA: Sage.

PART II

RESOURCES

4

THE DISCIPLINES CONSIDER SCHOLARSHIP

As part of a project undertaken by the Center for Instructional Development at Syracuse University and funded by the Lilly Endowment and the Fund for Improvement of Postsecondary Education, task forces from a number of professional/disciplinary associations have been working to consider ways in which the full range of faculty work can be recognized and valued within institutional reward systems. At this point, a number of those disciplinary groups have published statements proposing broader definitions of scholarly or professional work for their fields. The associations are at different points in the production of these statements which, when finalized, will be distributed to their memberships. Individual departments will be asked to use these statements to develop appropriate criteria for evaluating scholarly, intellectual or creative work within their own institutional contexts. As a way of displaying the range of responses to this challenge, we provide the following excerpts from the American Historical Association, The American Assembly of Collegiate Schools of Business, a consortium of associations representing faculty in the arts, the American Chemical Society, The Joint Policy Board for Mathematics, the American Academy of Religion, and the Association of American Geographers. Examples are meant to be illustrative and heuristic rather than definitive or comprehensive. A collection of the complete statements is published by: The American Association for Higher Education, 1 Dupont Circle, Suite 360, Washington, D.C. 20036.

Example 1

From the *American Historical Association Report*, December 1993

Adopting the Rice formulation of scholarship, the committee proposes that:

1. *The advancement of knowledge includes:*

   - Original research—based on manuscript and printed sources, material culture, oral history interviews, or other source materials—published in the form of a monograph or refereed journal article; or disseminated through a paper or lecture given at a meeting or conference or through a museum exhibition or other project or program; or presented in a contract research report, policy paper, or other commissioned study

   - Documentary or critical editions

   - Translations

2. *The integration of knowledge includes:*

   - Synthesis of scholarship—published in a review essay (journal or anthology), textbook, newsletter, popular history, magazine, encyclopedia, newspaper, or other form of publication; disseminated through a paper or lecture given at a meeting or conference or through a museum exhibition, film, or other public program; or presented in a contract research report, policy paper, or other commissioned study

   - Edited anthologies, journals, or series of volumes comprised of the work of other scholars

3. *The application of knowledge includes:*

   - Public history, specifically:

     Public programming (exhibitions, tours, etc.) in museums and other cultural and educational institutions

     Consulting and providing expert testimony on public policy and other matters

Contract research on policy formation and policy outcomes

Participation in film and other media projects

Writing and compiling institutional and other histories

Historic preservation and cultural resource management

Administration and management of historical organizations and institutions

Archival administration and the creation of bibliographies and databases

Professional services—editing journals and newsletters, organizing scholarly meetings, etc.

Community service drawing directly upon scholarship—through state humanities councils (e.g., public lectures), history day competitions, etc.

4. *The transformation of knowledge through teaching includes:*

- Student mentoring/advising

- Research, writing, and consulting in history education and in other disciplines allied to history

- Development of courses, curricula, visual materials, and teaching materials (including edited anthologies, textbooks, and software)—implemented in the classroom or disseminated through publications (books, professional newsletter articles, etc.), papers (annual meetings, teaching conferences, etc.), or non-print forms

- Organization and participation in collaborative content-based programs (workshops, seminars, etc.) with the schools

- Participation in developing and evaluating advanced placement and other forms of assessment

- Museum exhibitions, catalogues, film, radio, etc.—public programs as forms of teaching

Example 2

The *American Assembly of Collegiate Schools of Business*, June 1992

- *Basic scholarship: The creation of new knowledge*

  Outputs from basic scholarship activities include publication and refereed journals, research monographs, scholarly books, chapters in scholarly books, proceedings from scholarly meetings, papers presented at academic meetings, publicly available research working papers, and papers presented at faculty research seminars. Discovery research, the testing of theories, is included along with developing theories based on case development. Interdisciplinary work across fields, e.g., environmental studies and management, or language studies and international business, are also included.

- *Applied scholarship: The application, transfer, and interpretation of knowledge to approved management practice and teaching*

  Outputs from applied/service scholarship activities include publication and professional journals, professional presentations, public/trade/practitioner journals, in-house book reviews, and papers presented at faculty workshops. Also included are case writing to illustrate existing theories, adapting pure research of others into text, service to community, (e.g., internships and case enrichment), interpreting real world experience to classroom use that is generalizable and reusable, and interdisciplinary work across fields such as environmental studies in management or language studies and international business.

- *Instructional Development: The enhancement of the educational value of instructional efforts of the institution or discipline*

  Outputs from instructional development activities include textbooks, publications and pedagogical journals, written cases with instructional materials, instructional software, and publicly available materials describing the design and implementation of new courses. Also included are executive education course teaching, internships supervised by faculty, and materials used to enhance student learning, e.g., for advising and mentoring students and for assessment. In addition, developing new curriculum materials or support materials to be used by others (slides, video presentations, computer software, teachers' manuals) are included.

Example 3

From *The Work of the Theater Faculty*, from the National Office of Arts Accreditation in Higher Education, 1993

Creative Work and Research

Creating Theater

- Creating a work of theater: study, research, and synthesis that lead to original works, translations, interpretations, and adaptations (full-length and one-act plays, screenplays, children's theater); contribution and participation as a collaborative artist in the creation of theater

- Performing a work of theater: study, research, and practice that lead to live or broadcast performance, films or videos, including acting; directing; stage, costume, and lighting designing; technical directing; dramaturgy

Studying Theater and its Influences

- Analyzing how works of theater function: dramatic theory, criticism, interpretation

- Investigating and understanding the history and impact of theater: repertory; studies and analyses from historical, geographical, cultural, and other perspectives; history of ideas in theater; performance practices; bibliography; textual criticism and editing

- Researching the physiological and psychological impact of theater: perceptions of theatrical phenomena; relationship of theater to various specialized audiences; therapeutic applications

- Exploring the sociological impact of theater: theater and the human condition; theater and society; ethnographic and demographic studies; marketing

- Creating and assessing ideas and values about theater: aesthetics, criticism, and philosophy of theater

- Theater design and engineering

- Considering the multiple influences on theater from various sources: conditions, events, ideas, and technologies
- Integrating and synthesizing some or all of the above

Advancing the Pedagogy of Theater

- Developing instructional materials, curricula, and technologies that have broad impact on the field
- Determining causes and effects in education settings
- Integrating and applying theoretical and practical knowledge in educational policy settings
- Exploring philosophical, sociological, and historical connections between theater and education

Applying Theater and Facilitating Theater Activities

- Exploring and developing connections between theater and such areas as administration, commerce, public relations, therapies, and technologies: administration of presenting organizations and venues; artist and repertory management; theater-related industries; copyright; media arts
- Developing and practicing drama therapy
- Programming and publishing works of theater: designing or serving as artistic director of festivals; summer programs; theater series; workshops; master classes; seminars
- Exhibiting, programming, and publishing explanations, studies, and critiques; research and scholarly findings; translations and compilations: books and chapters in books; articles, monographs; delivering or publishing conference papers, panel discussions, proceedings; lectures; reviews of books, performances, productions, or new works of theater; appointments as artist-in-residence; performances as part of professional meetings; workshops; master classes, interviews; seminars; computer applications; program notes; exhibitions of stage and historical costume, stage designs, etc.

Example 4

The American Chemical Society, January 1993
Scholarship Areas

Research	Application
Discovery	Industrial interactions
Integration	Implementation of
Publications	new principles
Grants	Consulting
Monographs	Technology transfer
Teaching	**Outreach**
Classroom preparation	Scientific literacy
Curriculum development	K-12 enrichment
Graduate student	Extension service
training/education	Ethics
Textbooks	Minority/gender
Multimedia materials	recruitment/retention

Scholarship Criteria

Degree or extent of:

- Peer-reviewed publications—journal articles, books, or monographs
- Recognition by colleagues and organizations—invited papers, colloquia and awards
- Financial support—competitive peer-reviewed grants
  —industrial or home-institutional support

At the highest level of scholarship in a given area, there is publication in the most respected journals, international recognition, and substantial grant support. At the lowest level there is no communication with peers, no recognition outside the immediate activity, and no financial support. It is possible to reach the highest level of scholarship in any of the four areas listed, although it is most common to do so in the area of research. The task force recognizes the fact that mechanisms for gauging scholarship in areas outside of research are not generally or firmly in place. We encourage the creative development of new approaches to measure scholarship in chemistry across a broad spectrum of activities.

Example 5

From the *Joint Policy Board for Mathematics Report*, 1994

Defining Mathematical Scholarship

College and university faculty members are scholars as well as teachers. They must stay abreast of the latest developments in their fields in order to remain effective as teachers. Society looks to academia to advance the frontiers of knowledge and to communicate those advances not only to their students, but also to the larger public. Colleges and universities provide a particularly supportive environment for free inquiry, discovery, and the incubation of ideas. Academic scholars provide an important resource that can be drawn upon to address pressing local, regional, and national needs.

But what is scholarship? For some, scholarship is defined narrowly as research leading to new knowledge that is publishable in the leading research journals. Others define scholarship broadly as any activity that leads to increased knowledge or understanding on the part of the individual scholar. Between these two extremes is a variety of activities that may or may not be recognized as scholarly by those who make judgments about scholarship: deans, department chairs, colleagues and students, journal editors, and the public.

Each mathematical sciences department should formulate an explicit and public definition of scholarship that will inform its faculty members on the kinds of scholarly activity that are valued by the department, guide administrators and review committees that are charged with evaluating and rewarding that scholarship, and help all interested parties to understand the scholarly component of the departmental mission. This definition should, of course, be consistent with the mission of the institution. It should embrace the variety of scholarly activities in all fields that the institution and the department wish to encourage and support.

Following is a draft definition of scholarship for the mathematical sciences that may serve as a guide to departments seeking to formulate their own definitions. This draft will, of course, need to be modified by each department to reflect its own values and mission and to conform to the institutional mission.

Scholarship in the mathematical sciences includes:

- Research in core or applied areas that leads to new concepts, insights, discoveries, structures, theorems, or conjectures
- Research that leads to the development of new mathematical techniques, or new applications of known techniques, for addressing problems in other fields including the sciences, social sciences, medicine, and engineering
- Research in teaching and learning that leads to new insights into how mathematical knowledge and skills are most effectively taught and learned at all levels
- Synthesis, or integration, of existing scholarship, such as surveys, book reviews, and lists of open problems
- Exposition that communicates mathematics to new audiences, or to established audiences with improved clarity, either orally or in writing, including technical communications to scientists, engineers, and other mathematicians, as well as books, articles, multimedia materials and presentations for teachers, government leaders, and the general public
- Development of courses, curricula, or instructional materials for teaching mathematics in K–12 as well as at the college level
- Development of software that provides new or improved tools for supporting research in mathematics or its applications, for communicating mathematics, or for teaching and learning mathematics

Good scholarship, in whatever form it takes, must be shared in order to have value. It must benefit more than just the scholar. The results of scholarly activities must be public and must be amenable to evaluation. Techniques appropriate for the evaluation of scholarship in the mathematical sciences include peer review and invitations to present results to others; awards and other forms of recognition; and impact measure, such as citations, evidence of the use of scholarship in the work of others; evidence of improved effectiveness of a technique or activity as a result of the scholarly contribution, or evidence of improved effectiveness of a technique or activity as a result of the scholarly contribution, or evidence of improved understanding of mathematics on the part of some consumer groups as a result of the scholarly activity.

[Reprinted from the Joint Policy Board for Mathematics report, *Recognition and Rewards in the Mathematical Sciences*, with permission of the American Mathematical Society.]

Example 6

American Academy of Religion, 1994

Professional academic activity is based in scholarly intellectual and disciplined modes of knowing, and a commitment to creating, transmitting, expanding and transforming words of learning and understanding. The process emphasizes original, creative scholarship—including research in discovery, integration and reinterpretation; teaching; and service to the academic institution, the community, and the profession. While we cannot diminish, but should rather reaffirm the role of research as discovery, we must continue to challenge a framework of evaluation and reward that treats research and publication as the only valued intellectual activity. In the context of this report, however, we seek to revalorize teaching to acknowledge once more its importance in our profession, and to recommend that special attention be paid to professional service activity such as that which supports our relatively new public forum in the AAR.

Above all else, we seek to inspire and cultivate excellence in all three aspects of our academic activity. Excellence in teaching demands the best integrative and communicative skills as well as the imaginative capacity to foster the passion for learning, the ability to educe emerging ideas in one's students, and the skill to guide collective inquiry. Excellence in research reflects the highest quality work, notable in the following dimensions: innovation, integration, creativity, evidence of imagination, advanced language skills, mastery of a difficult area of study, contributions to the field, and communication of ideas. Excellence in service reveals a commitment to the discipline by way of an integration of personal, institutional and public service.

Our discussions on the evaluation and assessment of teaching have remained at the preliminary level, but we have concluded that, as noted above, we value the highest quality work and commitment in all dimensions of professional academic activity. We also emphasize the essential role of the process of peer review in evaluating the originality, scope, influence, and importance of each teacher-scholar's contributions.

Teaching

Professional academic activity in teaching is our daily lives, and forms the cornerstone for our discipline of religious studies. We teach in a field that studies both particular historical phenomena and ontological issues, engaging in philosophical studies, close reading of texts, investigation of social structures, and the meta-issues of postmodern thought. In the development of critical thinking, we bring our interdisciplinary approach to bear, challenging ourselves and our students not only to analyze our data but also to question the questions—and to ask difficult questions of other academic fields. While we begin with a shared fascination with the religious, some move to consider the most heartfelt issues in personal lives, while others focus on religious expression or seek to transform the understanding of religion itself. Teaching always continues beyond the classroom, and may reach beyond the institution and professional organizations as well. The appropriate means for the evaluation and assessment of teaching is grounded, again, in the wisdom of our peers; we must continue working to discover how to reward the already excellent teaching that religious studies professors do.

Teaching activities include (but are not limited to):

- Classroom teaching
- Computer-assisted teaching
- Directing internships
- Collaborating with students on research
- Student advising
- Curricular innovation: developing courses, course materials, software
- Development or restructuring of departmental, divisional, or university programs
- Development of new instructional techniques or pedagogies
- Research, writing, consulting in curriculum and development
- Participation in K-12 education and development of materials for such education
- Creation of public programs and issues seminars

- Course or curriculum assessment
- Bibliography or syllabus development for dissemination

Research

Original, creative research that advances knowledge is fundamental to our professional activity. Discovery, integration, and interpretation are part of the scholarly work that considers not only the marvelous details of specific case studies but also the history of study and evaluation of methodology. In whatever area we work, we note that the investigation of boundaries—of study, of culture areas, of perspectives, of methods—is critical to the very nature of religious studies fields. We take reflections on method and theory seriously, and have long grappled with interdisciplinary studies and cross-cultural sensibilities.

Preparation for research in religious studies often entails a broad spectrum of primary source work and linguistic studies, and the differential values of these across the discipline must not be ignored. Research is necessarily a transformative process, affecting the researcher in all dimensions of professional activity and the researcher's colleagues in our own and other fields. We cannot, then, simply measure outcomes by counting publications. Rather, excellence in research may be defined through peer review and evaluation of many kinds of research-related activities, focusing on the breadth and depth of influence. From this flows various responsibilities to our colleagues and institutions; central to these are our responsibility to represent the richness of religious studies research, to give and seek support within the existing reward systems, and to extend our transformed understandings to curriculum development. With the academy at large, scholars in religious studies must not evade but must attend to the evaluation and assessment of colleagues' research.

Research activities include (but are not limited to):

- Original research and theory/method development—disseminated (paper at meeting or conference; museum exhibit; other;) or published (journal article; book)
- Integration of scholarship in review essays, textbook, newsletter, popular publication, newspaper; through other public fora

- Edited anthologies, journals, dictionaries, sourcebooks
- Critical translations
- Critical editions of documents
- Grant writing
- Creation of teaching materials: manuals, workbooks, study guides, films
- Creation of computer software
- Bibliography development

Service

Professional academic activity in service normally begins in our departments, and extends to other levels of the university or college. Service to the profession, through the regional or national AAR or other professional organizations, supports the valued collegial network across which our research and teaching activities may also be encouraged and appreciated. Scholar/teachers in religious studies may also engage in outreach programs of at least two kinds. First, some may work in community outreach at the local, state or national levels, providing information on religions and religious studies or consulting on theory, methods or the central issues of study. Second, some may engage in "applied humanities" service, interpreting or helping make sense of the issues that confront the human community, reflecting the best ideas of the field. A scholar might, then, contribute to public discussion on war and peace, on the ethics of suffering, or on the religious history of suddenly-important groups. Excellence in service does not necessarily entail publication in scholarly, refereed journals; hence evaluation and assessment may consider the impact of the activity and its contribution to the enhancement of knowledge and interpretation in the wider sphere as well as to the recognition of our field.

Service activities include (but are not limited to):

- Department and campus committee work in standing, ad-hoc or other committees
- Consultancy to departmental or campus committees
- Department and campus leadership

- Student organization advising
- Advisory committees
- Professional service: editing journals, newsletters; organizing conferences; leadership in professional organizations
- Teaching workshops/peer review
- Recognition as national/regional authority
- Peer reviews of grants for foundations, articles for journals
- Course, curriculum, program or university assessment, both within one's institution and in service of others
- Electronic discussion development or management
- Community service, including public lectures or consultancy
- Consultancy with the media, textbook publishers, education groups
- Media appearances

Example 7

From *Reconsidering Faculty Roles and Rewards in Geography,* Association of American Geographers, 1994

We favor classifying faculty work into four roles that focus on the content of faculty activities in geography. We recognize that each institution has its own ways of defining faculty roles, some open and fluid, some highly circumscribed. In translating the terms we use, each geography program should adapt the concepts proposed below to the missions and nomenclatures prevalent in local evaluation and reward procedures. Where objectives and the ways faculty rewards are tied to them have not been articulated, that task should be given high priority.

Teaching

For the immediate future, classroom and laboratory instruction and thesis advising will continue to be central components of the teaching role. Professing geographers are employed by colleges and universities devoted to classroom instruction. Therefore, they will continue to draw upon their general knowledge of the discipline and appropriate lessons from their personal research to acquaint students in their introductory courses with how the world works geographically. They will use a different blend of general and personal perspectives to lead undergraduate majors and graduate students to progressively deeper understandings of the discipline, its links with other specialties, and its place in society. More often than not, these encounters will occur in traditional settings of classes, seminars, and thesis tutorials. For these teaching roles, traditional reward mechanisms, appropriately rebalanced, may suffice.

Yet teaching has many diverse facets in all kinds of academic institutions. Some of these dimensions common to most disciplines include:

- Advising undergraduates to design degree programs and evaluate career options.
- Supervising undergraduate senior research papers.
- Conceiving and implementing new courses and curricula.

- Developing and experimenting with innovative teaching approaches.
- Designing and teaching courses and programs that integrate geography with other disciplines.
- Initiating and participating in cooperative curriculum programs with other institutions.
- Establishing and supervising student internships.
- Adapting computer equipment and software to curriculum needs and integrating computer-assisted instruction into curricula.

Some tasks that are particularly important in geography are:

- Preparing for and serving in foreign studies programs.
- Instructing K-12 teachers (especially important in geography because until recently, virtually no students entered college or university intending to major in geography, and because of the emphasis on upgrading secondary school geography in the 1990s).
- Preparing for and conducting frequent and extended field trips.
- Winning funding for the specialized computer equipment that is increasingly prerequisite to responsible instruction in geography, and then setting up and maintaining the laboratories containing that equipment.
- Teaching cartography, which demands more time per student than most courses, because it can be taught well only tutorially.

Teaching geography involves instructing audiences well beyond traditional, intramural, tuition-paying students. Geographers often find their expertise sought in venues that impose special demands of time and intellectual commitment, demands that should be recognized in faculty evaluation and reward schemes. Faculty increasingly are called upon to convey information and decision-making approaches to the larger communities that provide their students and support their institutions. (The range of such teaching opportunities will be elaborated later in the section on outreach.)

Faculty, academic officers, and those who pay the bills for higher education will be more satisfied with faculty reward outcomes if all teaching roles are subjected to peer review. Restricting reward system purviews to traditional classroom and thesis advising responsibilities would be shortsighted, particularly in light of the opportunities for innovative, computer-based, self-instruction that will emerge in the next decade.

Research

Research in geography encompasses three forms of creative work:

- Geographers engage in *basic* research to produce or discover new knowledge about the world we inhabit and the ways it functions. In that effort, geographers use an unusual number of conceptual and analytical approaches, drawn from the earth sciences, the behavioral and social sciences, and the humanities. We include in our definition of basic research in geography attempts to enhance the distinctive methods geographers use in their work: cartography, geographic information systems, remote sensing, and spatial statistics.

- Geographers who pursue *synthesizing* research seek to (1) combine basic research findings from across the remarkably large number of subfields within the discipline, (2) integrate results from cognate disciplines into geographical analysis and theory, and (3) merge existing and new knowledge about a place or a region into a cohesive portrayal of that area, either as an entity of intrinsic interest or as the locus of a topical phenomenon or problem.

- Academic geographers engaged in *applied* research (as distinct from geographers who *practice* in the private and public sectors) focus on solving societal problems. They may pose the issues they address, or they may respond to challenges that arise in relevant agencies, firms, or industries. Although geographers who prefer applied research often apply the results of basic research to extramural problems, ideas flow in both directions between basic and applied research. Basic questions often arise in the course of trying to solve a seemingly straightforward practical problem.

As noted earlier, geographers who can demonstrate proficiency in basic research have an inside track in winning professional recognition and the tangible rewards that accompany it. Those who concentrate on synthesizing and applied research often must work harder and longer for equivalent rewards, even though synthesizing and applied research long have been embedded in the geographic research tradition.

Basic research will persist as a foundation for other kinds of research in geography. Accordingly, geographers should continue to value it highly, evaluate its quality rigorously, and reward it appropriately. However that priority does not imply that basic research should continue to be accorded its traditional weight relative to synthesizing and applied research. Integration and application deserve greater returns than have customarily accrued to them. To achieve that rebalancing, the products of synthesis and application must be subjected to the same intense peer evaluation that is used to assess basic research.

Outreach

Service often has been used as a catchall category to encompass work not clearly included under the traditional rubrics of teaching and research. We prefer to characterize the third major role geographers play as *outreach*. Outreach in geography includes, among other activities:

- Responding to requests to undertake applied research projects.
- Consulting in the public and private sectors.
- Helping improve geography instruction in primary, secondary, and postsecondary schools.
- Explaining one's discipline or research using mass media.
- Writing for lay audiences.
- Testifying as an expert in legislative or judicial settings.
- Lecturing to the public.
- Serving on boards and commissions that draw upon and enhance disciplinary and professional expertise.

Geographers deal with the world as it exists and as it might be. They have much of great value to say about environmental and human problems across a spectrum of analytical scales ranging from localities to the globe. In lending their energies to those problems in ways that draw upon and exercise their expertise, geographers fulfill a mandate implicit in the intellectual heritage they cultivate. Accordingly, outreach should be valued more highly than it has been in most academic institutions since World War II. Individual programs will accord outreach different weights when striking their own balances among faculty roles, but more incentives for faculty to undertake outreach would yield worthwhile dividends, including:

- Greater visibility resulting from the appreciation by decision-makers and the public of contributions by geographers to the solution of societal problems.

- Augmented theoretical development engendered by the propensity of the world to work contrary to theory-based expectations.

- Enhanced faculty proficiency in teaching and research as a result of grappling with substantive problems.

- Laboratory and field experience for students, including internships.

- Increased financial support for students and equipment based on better knowledge of agency and industry needs and funding opportunities.

Geography's strong empirical and exploratory traditions and its rootedness in real places and regions often lead geographers to devote considerable energy and time to outreach. The ability and propensity of geographers to grapple with real problems is a disciplinary strength and an institutional asset. Geography programs should ensure that their departmental and institutional reward systems weight such contributions appropriately.

Citizenship

Citizenship obligations accompany every professorial appointment. One way faculty members exercise citizenship is by service within their programs or departments. As the term implies, all faculty members should take some share of common responsibilities. Within any program, tasks should be allocated as needed for the ongoing functioning of the organization. Citizenship at the institutional scale maintains a program's visibility on campus, and individual faculty members also must assume an appropriate share of such corporate responsibilities. Occasionally, citizenship within an institution may draw upon a faculty member's geographical expertise in the same way that local bodies may call upon it. Occasionally, exceptionally large citizenship commitments may be required without significant work reduction, such as presiding over a faculty senate or chairing a major university task force. On such occasions, recognition beyond that accorded to expected levels of citizenship should be given.

A second arena in which faculty members discharge citizenship responsibilities is their disciplines. Faculty reasonably can be expected to review journal manuscripts and research proposals, advise extramural colleagues on work in progress, write letters of recommendation for students and for colleagues, and accept appointments to the committees of scholarly societies. As with institutional citizenship, disciplinary service sometimes may require extraordinary commitments that warrant special recognition; an example would be serving as president of a scholarly society.

The fulfillment of *civic* responsibilities should not be confused with professorial citizenship. However laudable, an activity that is not grounded in disciplinary knowledge, faculty role expertise, or both, has no place in faculty reward evaluations. Speaking about geography to your daughter's elementary school class during Geography Awareness Week may be an instance of citizenship; speaking to your daughter's class about your hobby is not.

5

STUDENT RATINGS OF FACULTY: SPECIAL INSTRUCTIONAL SETTINGS
(SELECTED EXAMPLES)

Laboratory

- To what extent did the assignments relate to course concepts?
- Were the laboratory activities coordinated with other work in the course?
- Was the instructor prepared for laboratory sessions and pre-activity discussions?
- Were you provided with adequate instructions for proceeding with your laboratory exercises?
- Did you have enough time in the laboratory to complete your exercises?

Studio

- Were you exposed to a variety of techniques and procedures?
- Did the instructor take time to work with you individually?
- Were the instructor's examples/demonstrations clear and concise?
- Did you have enough time to develop the skills you needed to succeed?
- Were the instructor's critiques of your work useful? Did you learn from them?

- Was the instructor sensitive to your problems?
- Did your instructor help you think about different ways to approach projects?

Team-Teaching

- Did one instructor dominate the course?
- Were the faculty involved in teaching the course compatible with each other?
- Did the involvement of more than one faculty member provide you with insights that a single faculty could not?
- Was the instruction in the course coordinated?

Internship/Clinical

- Were you exposed to a variety of problems?
- Was the experience realistic?
- Were your questions thoroughly answered?
- Were problems clearly stated?
- Was evaluation consistent?
- Were appropriate and inappropriate clinical procedures/ approaches clearly identified and discussed?

These examples are based on items included in the *Instructor and Course Evaluation System,* Office of Instructional Resources, Measurement, and Research Division, University of Illinois at Urbana-Champaign.

6

EVALUATING TEACHING: SELECTED ADDITIONAL REFERENCES

A faculty guide for relating public service to the promotion and tenure review process. (1993). Urbana, IL: University of Illinois at Urbana-Champaign, Office of Continuing Education and Public Service.

Boyer, E. (1990). *Scholarship reconsidered: Priorities for the professoriate.* Princeton, NJ: Carnegie Foundation for the Advancement of Teaching.

Braskamp, L.A., & Ory, J. C. (1994). *Assessing faculty work.* San Francisco, CA: Jossey-Bass.

Centra, J.A. (1979). *Determining faculty effectiveness.* San Francisco, CA: Jossey-Bass.

Centra, J.A. (1994). *Reflective faculty evaluation.* San Francisco, CA: Jossey-Bass.

Diamond, R.M., & Adam, B.E. (1993). *Recognizing faculty Work: Reward systems for the year 2000. 81.* San Francisco, CA: Jossey-Bass.

Edgerton, R., Hutchings, P., & Quinlan, K. (1991). *The teaching portfolio: Capturing the scholarship in teaching.* Washington, DC: American Association for Higher Education.

Elman, S.E., & Smock, S.M. (1985). *Professional service and faculty rewards.* Washington, DC: National Association of State Universities and Land-Grant Colleges.

Hutchings, P. (1993). *Campus use of the teaching portfolio: Twenty-five profiles*. Washington, DC: American Association for Higher Education.

Rice, E. (1991). The new American scholar: Scholarship and the purposes of the university. *Metropolitan Universities Journal.*

Seagren, A.T., Creswell, J.T., & Wheeler, D.W. (1993). *The department chair: New roles, responsibilities and challenges*. ASHE-ERIC Higher Education Report No 1. Washington, DC: The George Washington University, School of Education and Human Development.

Seldin, P. (1984). *Changing practices in faculty evaluation*. San Francisco, CA: Jossey-Bass.

Seldin, P. (1991). *The teaching portfolio*. Bolton, MA: Anker.

Seldin, P. (1993). *Successful use of the teaching portfolio*. Bolton, MA: Anker.

Shulman, L. (1989). Toward a pedagogy of substance. *AAHE Bulletin*. Washington, DC: American Association for Higher Education.

7

Evaluating an Advisor:
Selected Items from the ACT
Survey of Academic Advising

		DOES NOT APPLY	STRONGLY AGREE	AGREE	NEUTRAL	DISAGREE	STRONGLY DISAGREE
19.	Allows sufficient time to discuss issues or problems.	O	O	O	O	O	O
20.	Is willing to discuss personal problems.	O	O	O	O	O	O
21.	Anticipates my needs.	O	O	O	O	O	O
22.	Helps me select courses that match my interests and abilities.	O	O	O	O	O	O
23.	Helps me to examine my needs, interests, and values.	O	O	O	O	O	O
24.	Is familiar with my academic background.	O	O	O	O	O	O
25.	Encourages me to talk about myself and my college experiences.	O	O	O	O	O	O
26.	Encourages my interest in an academic discipline.	O	O	O	O	O	O
27.	Encourages my involvement in extracurricular activities.	O	O	O	O	O	O
28.	Helps me explore careers in my field of interest.	O	O	O	O	O	O
29.	Is knowledgeable about courses outside my major area of study.	O	O	O	O	O	O
30.	Seems to enjoy advising.	O	O	O	O	O	O
31.	Is approachable and easy to talk to.	O	O	O	O	O	O
32.	Shows concern for my personal growth and development.	O	O	O	O	O	O
33.	Keeps personal information confidential.	O	O	O	O	O	O
34.	Is flexible in helping me plan my academic program.	O	O	O	O	O	O
35.	Has a sense of humor.	O	O	O	O	O	O
36.	Is a helpful, effective advisor whom I would recommend to other students.	O	O	O	O	O	O

For information on the use of this instrument contact:
American College Testing Program
P.O. Box 168
Iowa City, IA 52243
(319) 337-1000

8

DOCUMENTING AND ASSESSING WORK OF FACULTY:
SELECTED EXAMPLES

Author Textbook as Fundamental Introduction to the Discipline

Rationale

- Demonstrates high level of understanding of the field, ability to integrate knowledge, plus ability to represent knowledge to others (and thus a teaching skill)
- May represent knowledge that is put together in creative or novel ways leading to new insights
- Integrates teaching and scholarly aspects of faculty role
- Has potential for leading to future scholarship
- Makes teaching public—cosmopolitan—beyond bounds of campus
- Helps other faculty think of different ways of organizing and presenting information

Guidelines for Documentation

Evidence

- Descriptive essay—should include a statement of existing need and a discussion of how the text represents a new approach or paradigm
- Product itself
- Reviews from publisher (during selection process)

- Published reviews
- Student assessments
- Sales (overall and by institution and type)
- Citations (where appropriate)

Criteria

- Marketability; fills important or unique niche; levels of adoption
- Quality, accuracy, clarity of content (peers)
- Presentation, style, learning impact (students)
- Impact on how subject is taught
- Degree of innovation (structure, content, and/or presentation)
- Epistemological impact; how knowledge is structured

Develop New High School Curriculum

Rationale

- Demonstrates the ability to communicate important concepts to a diverse population
- Can increase general student interest in the field
- Can prepare students for further study in the discipline
- Can represent a major new approach to education in the discipline

Guidelines for Documentation

Evidence

- Descriptive essay—including statement of need, goals of the project, and rationale for approach being used
- Reviews by experts in the field (college and secondary) and by teachers who are using the materials produced
- The materials
- Data on changes in student learning and attitudes
- Data on feasibility of continued and expanded use (cost, etc.)

Criteria

- Represents a major innovation
- Quality and accuracy of content
- Meets specific needs of student population being served
- Has application beyond test site (adoption by other schools)
- Validated by an independent review process

Direct a Play (Student Production)

Rationale

- Can represent a new interpretation of the work
- Requires disciplinary expertise and an historical frame of reference
- Requires the ability to make maximum use of existing resources (human and material)
- Provides theory/practice application for students in cast and serving in other production-related roles (teaching function)

Guidelines for Documentation

Evidence

- Descriptive essay—includes a statement of production goals, a description of the process that was followed, and a rationale for the decisions that were made
- Videotape of final production for external peer review
- Critical reviews
- Audience response
- Students' written reflections and critique

Criteria

- Shows evidence of high level of disciplinary expertise
- Makes maximum use of existing resources
- Production is innovative; breaks new ground
- Demonstrates student learning

Design a New Course

Rationale

- Requires a high level of disciplinary expertise
- Can have major impact on student motivation, learning, retention, and attitudes toward the field of study. Can also increase interest of high quality students to major in field
- By improving learning, meets the stated goals of department, school, college, and institution
- Can help prepare students for other courses in the field and for successful careers

Guidelines for Documentation

Evidence

- Descriptive essay—includes statement of needs and rationale for design
- Syllabi or student manuals
- Newly created course materials
- Video of class presentation (of innovative teaching strategies)
- Student ratings
- Student performance data (tests and test results). Focus, if appropriate, on specific population
- Comments regarding student preparation from faculty teaching high level courses in the discipline
- Reviews of course and materials by experts in field (faculty and/or professionals)
- Results of field tests and revisions based on this data
- Comparative data on retention, class attendance, number of students selecting further study in the field

Criteria

- Shows high level of disciplinary expertise
- Represents an innovation or new approach in design, delivery, or content that can be replicated

- Learning outcomes are clearly stated and match the course objectives
- Meets needs of student population being served and stated instructional goals
- Is approved by department and curriculum committee

Serve on Community Task Force
Appointed by City Mayor

Rationale

- Requires high level of disciplinary expertise
- Can have major impact on reducing conflict within the community
- Fits within institutional mission statement regarding community service
- Can be used as a case study for classroom use or further research

Guidelines for Documentation

Evidence

- Reflective essay—describe problems being faced, role of the faculty member and what faculty member learned or discovered
- Description of specific actions faculty member took as part of task force and reasons for those choices
- Transcripts or minutes of task force meetings
- Letters of commendation by task force chair or members
- Written testimony from community groups who benefited from the work of the task force
- Course materials developed from this case
- Student interaction with faculty members' work or responses to case
- Institutional or unit goal statement articulating community service mission
- Committee interviews with key actors, mayor, community leaders, etc.
- Results of work of task force as evidence of impact on community (i.e., specific initiatives planned and accomplished)
- Publication and dissemination of reports

Criteria

- Demonstrates high level of professional expertise
- Demonstrates knowledge of recent research in conflict resolution
- Demonstrates strong performance as task force member
- Demonstrates innovative solutions to common societal problems
- Demonstrates sensitivity to various constituencies
- Interest in results, outcomes by other communities
- Publication of accounts of activity in news and other media
- Publication of accounts in disciplinary journals

Assist Regional Museum in Producing an Exhibit on Indians of the American Southwest (Historian)

Rationale

- Requires a high level of disciplinary expertise
- Involves both original research and new conceptualization of the history and culture of the region
- Requires expertise in pedagogical theory and methodology
- Fits within the institutional mission of community service
- Fits within institutional mission to support cultural diversity

Guidelines for Documentation

Evidence

- Descriptive essay—describes problems being faced, the goals of the exhibit and its contributions to both research and teaching
- Exhibit script and related publications
- Statement of educational goals and report on visitor evaluation
- Peer reviews of exhibit

Criteria

- Shows high level of disciplinary expertise
- Is innovative in conceptualization and presentation
- Is instructionally effective
- Approach can be applied by others
- Demonstrates ability to work effectively as a team member
- Demonstrates ability to be sensitive to educational level of intended audience

Develop a Software System to Model
Storm Water Run-Off in Urban Environments

Rationale

- Addresses a major environmental problem
- Demonstrates a high level of disciplinary expertise
- Demonstrates a high level of competence in computer programming
- Demonstrates a high level of competence in environmental modeling
- By improving the design process, can reduce costs, improve decision-making, improve safety, reduce flood damage

Guidelines for Documentation

Evidence

- Software package, including manual which details assumptions, limitations, etc.
- Descriptive essay—should describe problems being faced (i.e., statement of need), design rationale, benefits of the system, and what makes it an innovative approach
- Published reports and statements for users
- Data on applications (number of users and range of applications)
- Research data on impact (cost reductions in design, savings from reduced damage, etc.)

Criteria

- Marketability meets a defined need
- Quality of the system (external reviews)
- Adaptations and use of the system (national and international use)
- Impact of use (reduced costs, reduction in damage, etc.)
- Degree of innovation

9

PREPARING FOR PROMOTION AND TENURE: A FACULTY CHECKLIST

Basic Requirements

☐ Have you included all the items required by your department, school/college guidelines?

Cover Letter or Faculty Essay

Does your cover letter or faculty essay provide guidelines that will help the committee review your materials? Have you discussed:

☐ the significance of your work from your perspective?

☐ the challenges you faced and what you accomplished?

☐ the decisions you made and why you made them?

☐ the circumstances that promoted or inhibited success?

☐ the rationale for the materials you have included in your documentation?

☐ the relationship of your work to the priorities of your department, school/college, institution, and discipline?

Teaching

In documenting the quality of your teaching have you:

☐ presented evidence of quality planning and course design (course organization)?

☐ presented evidence of student learning?

☐ included student ratings showing comparison with other faculty?

☐ included student ratings showing evidence of improvement (where appropriate)?

☐ showed evidence of effective, appropriate instructional techniques?

☐ showed evidence of positive impact on retention?

Scholarly/Professional/Creative Work

☐ If you have conducted research and/or published, have you documented the quality and the significance of this work?

☐ Have you included statements from qualified external reviewers?

☐ If appropriate, have you included videos of performance or related activities or included other appropriate visual materials?

☐ If you have developed innovative instructional materials or written a textbook, have you included external reviews or student performance data that address both the significance and the quality of your work?

Advising

☐ Have you documented the quality of your advising?

Community Service

☐ Have you documented service, outreach or citizenship (department, school/college, institution, community)?

General

☐ Have you eliminated all redundant material?

☐ Have you prepared your material in a way that will communicate effectively with colleagues from other disciplines?

☐ Have you included a Table of Contents to assist the committee in locating specific items?

☐ Have you had someone else review your materials?